T0204969

Dolphins

Melissa Stewart

NATIONAL
GEOGRAPHIC

Washington, D.C.

For Claire
—M.S.

Published by National Geographic Partners, LLC, Washington, DC 20036.

Library of Congress Cataloging-in-Publication Data
Stewart, Melissa.
Dolphins / Melissa Stewart.
p. cm.
ISBN 978-1-4263-0652-5 (pbk. : alk. paper) — ISBN 978-1-4263-0653-2 (library binding : alk. paper)
1. Dolphins—Juvenile literature. I. Title.
QL737.C432S73 2010
599.53—dc22
2009022832

Cover, Daniel Hussey/iStockphoto/Getty Images; 1, Stephen Frink/Getty Images; 2, Mauricio Handler; 4-5, Konrad Wothe/Minden Pictures; 6, Carlos Eyles; 7, David B. Fleetham/Blue Planet Archive; 8-9, Brandon Cole; 10, Carlos Eyles; 12-13, Doug Perrine/Blue Planet Archive; 14, Wolcott Henry/National Geographic Image Collection; 15, Miriam Stein; 16, Hiroya Minakuchi/Minden Pictures; 18-19, Doug Perrine/Blue Planet Archive; 19, Ingrid Visser/Blue Planet Archive; 20, Florian Graner/Nature Picture Library; 20 (inset), Uko Gorter; 21, Doug Perrine/Blue Planet Archive; 21 (inset), Uko Gorter; 22, Kevin Schafer; 23, Todd Pusser/Nature Picture Library; 24, Michael S. Nolan/Blue Planet Archive; 25 (UP), Joao Quaresma/Blue Planet Archive; 25 (LO), Roland Seitre/Blue Planet Archive; 26-27, Brandon Cole; 28-29, A. L. Stanzani/ARDEA; 29 (UP), Phillip Colla/Blue Planet Archive; 29 (CTR), Doug Perrine/Blue Planet Archive; 29 (LO), Kevin Schafer/National Geographic Image Collection; 31, Bob Couey-SeaWorld via Getty Images; 32 (UP LE), Brandon Cole; 32 (UP RT), NG Maps; 32 (CTR LE), A. L. Stanzani/ARDEA; 32 (CTR RT), A. L. Stanzani/ARDEA; 32 (LO LE), Carlos Eyles; 32 (LO RT), Doug Perrine/Blue Planet Archive

Printed in South Korea
24/ISK/1

Table of Contents

It's a Dolphin!

What swims
in the water,
but isn't a fish?

What whistles
and chirps,
but isn't a bird?

What loves to jump,
but isn't a frog?

It's a **DOLPHIN!**

Fish or Mammal?

A dolphin is a mammal—just like you.

Dolphins have lungs and breathe air. They get oxygen through a hole on top of their heads.

Their tails move up and down.

They have soft, smooth skin.

A dolphin's body temperature is always about 97 degrees Fahrenheit.

OXYGEN:
An invisible gas
in air and water
that animals
breathe in.

MAMMAL:
A warm-blooded
animal that drinks
milk from its
mother and has a
backbone
and hair.

Dolphins look like
fish, but they are different in some
very important ways.

Fish have scales.

Fish have
gills. Gills
help fish get
oxygen from
the water.

Their tails bend from side to side.

A fish's body temperature matches the
temperature of the water it's in.

A Dolphin's Life

A baby dolphin
is called a calf.

A baby dolphin has a small
mouth. The calf smacks
food against the water to
break it into bite-size bits.

A calf can swim as soon as it is born. It drinks milk from its mother's body. When the little dolphin is about six months old, it starts to eat fish.

Water Words

CALF:
A young dolphin

9

A dolphin pod

Dolphins live in small groups called pods. Some pods join together to form schools. A dolphin school may have more than 1,000 animals.

Dolphins use squeaks, squeals, and whistles to "talk" to each other. Some dolphins in a pod are in charge of watching for sharks and other predators.

Every dolphin has its own name. Each name is a series of whistling sounds.

Water Words

PREDATOR: Animals that eat other animals

Dolphins work together to catch prey. Dolphin pods will swim circles around a school of fish until the fish are tightly packed together.

Water Words

PREY: Animals that are eaten by other animals

This big group of fish is called a "bait ball." When the fish have nowhere to escape, the dolphins take turns diving in for a snack.

13

Under the Sea

A dolphin's body is just right for life underwater.

Flippers help a dolphin start, stop, and turn.

The fin on a dolphin's back helps it stay balanced.

Its powerful tail pushes it through the water.

When a dolphin swims slowly,
it rises to the surface and breathes
once or twice a minute. When a
dolphin swims fast, it leaps out
of the water to catch its breath.

Blowhole

When a dolphin breathes out, air blasts out of its
blowhole at 100 miles an hour.

Dolphins have great eyesight, but the ocean can be very dark. It's hard for dolphins to see the little fish they like to eat on the ocean floor.

If a dolphin is hunting alone, it will put its head to the ground and make a clicking noise.

The noise hits anything in the dolphin's path and bounces back. A dolphin can find a fish by seeing it with sound!

This dolphin is using echolocation. You say it like this: eck oh low kay shun. Dolphins actually use echoes to locate the fish they can't see.

Where Dolphins Live

More than 30 different kinds of dolphins live on Earth.

Most dolphins swim in warm ocean waters near the Equator. But some live in cooler seas north and south of the Equator, and some even live in rivers.

The hourglass dolphin lives way out in the middle of the ocean.

The Hector's dolphin usually stays close to land.

Water Words

EQUATOR: An imaginary line halfway between the North and South Poles.

What's the Difference?

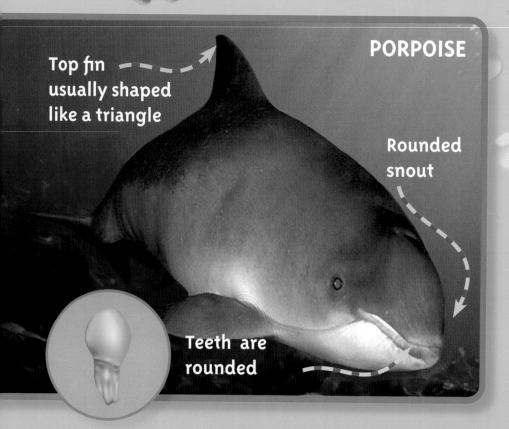

PORPOISE

Top fin usually shaped like a triangle

Rounded snout

Teeth are rounded

Have you ever seen a porpoise? It looks like a dolphin, but it's different. You say it like this: poor pus.

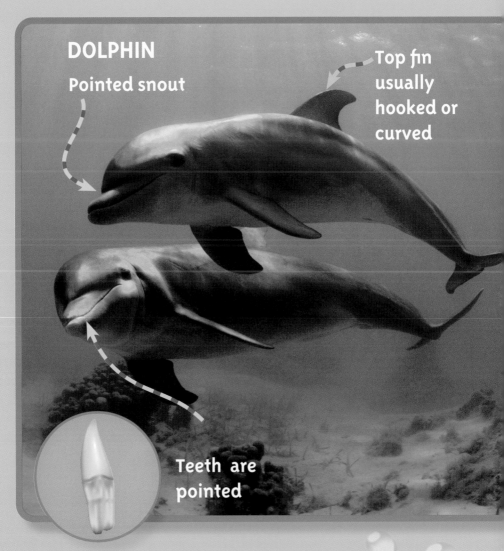

DOLPHIN

Pointed snout

Top fin usually hooked or curved

Teeth are pointed

A dolphin's body is longer and leaner than a porpoise's body. Dolphins are more curious and playful, too.

21

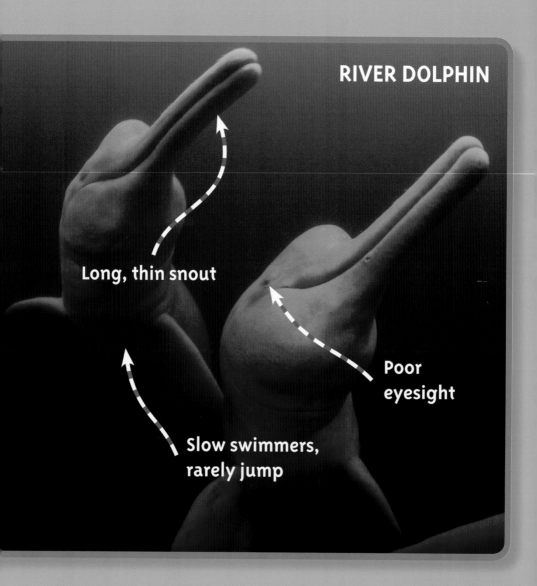

RIVER DOLPHIN

Long, thin snout

Poor eyesight

Slow swimmers, rarely jump

Have you ever seen a dolphin with a long pointy snout? This funny looking mammal is a river dolphin.

OCEAN DOLPHIN

Good eyesight

Short snout

Fast swimmers,
often jump

River dolphins are smaller than
their ocean-swimming cousins. They
are also less active and playful.

Super Dolphins

SUPER SPINNER

A spinner dolphin twirls through the air like a spiraling football. It can jump almost ten feet into the air and spin up to seven times.

Q What is a spinner dolphin's favorite amusement park ride?

A The merry-go-round.

EASY BREATHER

A dolphin spends most of its life holding its breath. A Risso's dolphin can go for 30 minutes without coming up for air.

DEEPEST DIVER

Whales and dolphins are very closely related. In fact, some animals we call whales really are dolphins. The long-finned pilot whale is a dolphin that can dive almost 2,000 feet!

The most amazing dolphin of all is the **ORCA,** also known as the killer whale. The orca wins almost every record-setting award in the dolphin category.

A killer whale can swim seven times faster than an Olympic swimmer!

Q What did the ocean say to the killer whale when it left on vacation?

Nothing. It just waved. **A**

HUNGRIEST
An orca eats everything from sea turtles and penguins to seals and sharks.

LONGEST LIVING
A killer whale can live up to 90 years.

BIGGEST
Males can grow almost as long as a school bus.

Goofing Off

Dolphins spend a lot of time hunting for food. And they are always on the lookout for danger. But sometimes dolphins just want to have fun. Dolphins make up all kinds of games.

PLAYING CATCH: Toss seaweed into the air and try to catch it.

SURFING: Ride along storm waves or waves breaking near a beach.

TAG, YOU'RE IT: Chase each other through the water.

Dolphins and Humans

Dolphins are gentle, playful creatures. They are also very smart, which is why people and dolphins get along so well.

By learning about these friendly marine mammals, humans are helping to protect dolphins and the waters they live in.

Q What is a dolphin's favorite TV show?

A Whale of Fortune!

CALF: A young dolphin

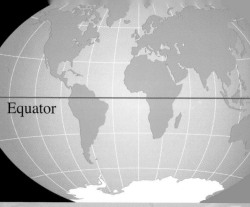

Equator

EQUATOR: An imaginary line halfway between the North and South Poles

MAMMAL: A warm-blooded animal that drinks its mother's milk, has a backbone, and hair.

OXYGEN: An invisible gas in air and water. It helps animals get energy from food.

PREDATOR: Animals that eat other animals

PREY: Animals that are eaten by other animals

Manatees

LEVEL 2

Laura Marsh

NATIONAL GEOGRAPHIC

Washington, D.C.

For Paul —L.F.M.

The publisher and author gratefully acknowledge the expert review
of this book by Deborah Epperson, Ph.D.

Published by National Geographic Partners, LLC, Washington, DC 20036.

Book design by YAY! Design

Trade paperback ISBN: 978-1-4263-1472-8
Reinforced library binding ISBN: 978-1-4263-1473-5

Table of Contents

Who Am I?

I have whiskers,
but I am not a cat.

I nibble on grass,
but I am not a cow.

I have gray, wrinkled
skin, but I am not an
elephant.

Who am I?
A manatee!

Mighty Manatees

Manatees often rest in groups.

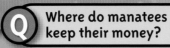
Manatees are mammals that live in the water. They are sometimes called "sea cows."

Why?

Manatees are gentle and they move slowly, like cows. They also graze on sea grass, just like cows eat grass.

Water Words

MAMMAL: An animal that has a backbone and is warm-blooded. It feeds its babies milk.

GRAZE: To feed in an area covered with grasses

Manatees are big. They are usually about ten feet long. That's as long as two kids' bikes lined up end to end.

Manatees are heavy, too.
Most adult manatees weigh about
1,000 pounds. That's the weight
of about 21 second graders!

Super Swimmers

Manatees can move their large bodies gracefully through the water. They swim upside down and roll. They even do somersaults (SUM-ur-sawlts)!

Q Why are manatees so wrinkled?

A Because they do not use irons!

A group of manatees swims in Crystal River, Florida, U.S.A.

Manatees don't like water that is too deep. They like to stay in shallow water in oceans and rivers. There, they find food and warm water.

A manatee's body is built for living in the water.

TAIL: It is large, flat, and round at the end. It moves up and down to power the manatee through the water.

EYES: They are small, but manatees can see well, even in cloudy water.

NOSTRILS: Manatees breathe air through these holes. But they close tightly underwater.

FLIPPERS: They help steer the manatee. They also bring food to its mouth.

LIPS: They are big and strong. They wrap around plants and pull them into the manatee's mouth.

Munching on Lunch

Manatees are herbivores (HUR-buh-vores). They eat plants for about six to eight hours every day.

A manatee grazes on sea plants.

Manatees have no front teeth. They don't need them because they don't eat meat.

Manatees have only large back teeth called molars. The molars help grind their food.

Water Word

HERBIVORE: An animal that eats only plants

7 Fun Facts About Manatees

1 They lose teeth all through their lives. New teeth replace them.

2 The elephant is a distant relative of the manatee.

3 Fat in the mother's milk helps a young manatee grow quickly.

4

They do not have eyelashes.

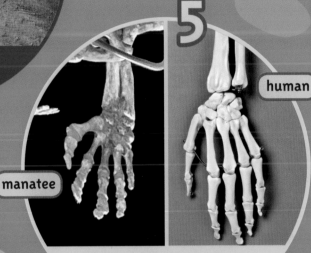

5

human

manatee

Bones in a manatee's flipper are similar to those in a human hand.

6

They do not use their mouth to breathe. They only use their nostrils.

7

They have no natural enemies. Humans are their biggest threat.

Big Babies

These young manatees are fed milk from a bottle. Without their mothers, they need help to eat.

A manatee baby is called a calf.
It is born underwater. A newborn
calf is about the size of a nine-
year-old kid.

The mother pushes the calf to
the surface to take its first breath.
Within an hour, the calf can
swim on its own.

Like other mammal babies, a manatee drinks its mother's milk. Soon it learns how to find sea grasses to eat.

A calf needs to stick with its mom.

The calf must stay with its mother for the first two years. The mother teaches her calf how to live on its own.

On the Move

Manatees do not stay in one place. They migrate (MY-grate).

In summer, manatees can be found in many states. In winter, most manatees return to Florida. The water is warmer there.

Water Word

MIGRATE: To move from one area to another for food or a mate

North America

UNITED STATES

FLORIDA

50°

40°

U

S

TEXAS

30°

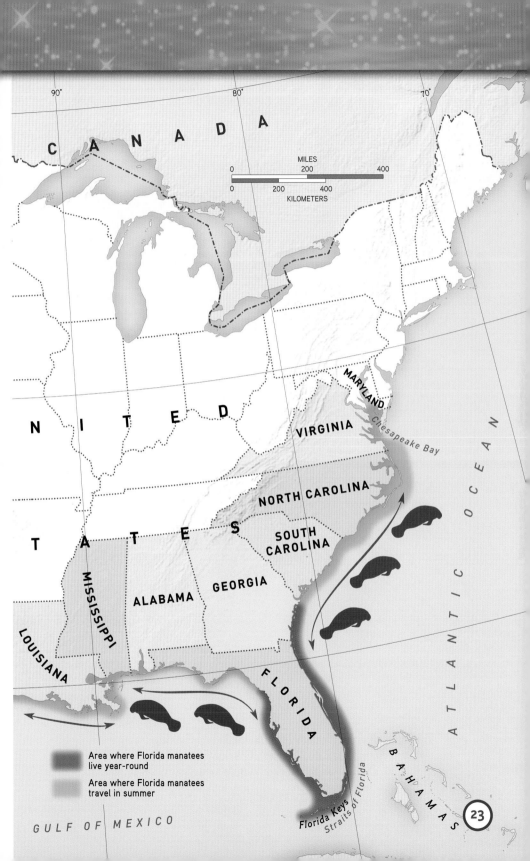

90°   80°   70°

C A N A D A

MILES
0   200   400
0   200   400
KILOMETERS

U N I T E D

MARYLAND
Chesapeake Bay

VIRGINIA

NORTH CAROLINA

SOUTH
CAROLINA

S T A T E S

MISSISSIPPI

ALABAMA   GEORGIA

LOUISIANA

F L O R I D A

A T L A N T I C   O C E A N

Area where Florida manatees
live year-round

Area where Florida manatees
travel in summer

B A H A M A S

Florida Keys
Straits of Florida

GULF OF MEXICO

23

Manatees at Rest

Manatees don't usually travel in groups.
But they often rest together in warm water.

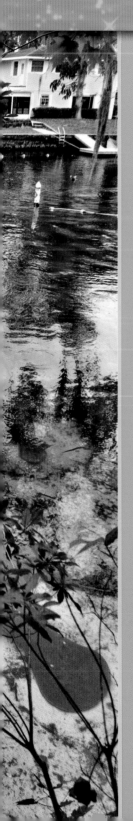

Manatees need rest, like you. But they don't sleep like you do.

They rest for about 15 minutes at a time. Then they need to come to the surface to breathe.

Manatees sometimes rest at the bottom of the sea or river. They can also float near the top of the water when resting.

25

Keeping Manatees Safe

There are many dangers for manatees. They are often hit by boats because they are big and slow and swim near the surface. Manatees can be hard to see in the water.

Manatee Zone
SLOW SPEED
MINIMUM WAKE
Sep 1 - Apr 30
35 MPH Day 25MPH Night
May 1 - Aug 31

This manatee has scars from an injury by a boat propeller.

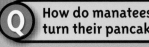

People also throw trash and fishing line into the water. Swallowing trash can hurt manatees. Fishing line can get tangled around manatees so they can't swim.

27

Manatees are endangered
(in-DANE-jurd).
There are about 5,000
Florida manatees left.

But laws protect them.
There are also special
areas for manatees called
sanctuaries (SANGK-choo-
er-eez). In a sanctuary,
people can't disturb
manatees. They can live
safely there and raise
their young.

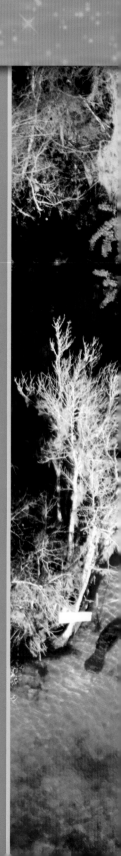

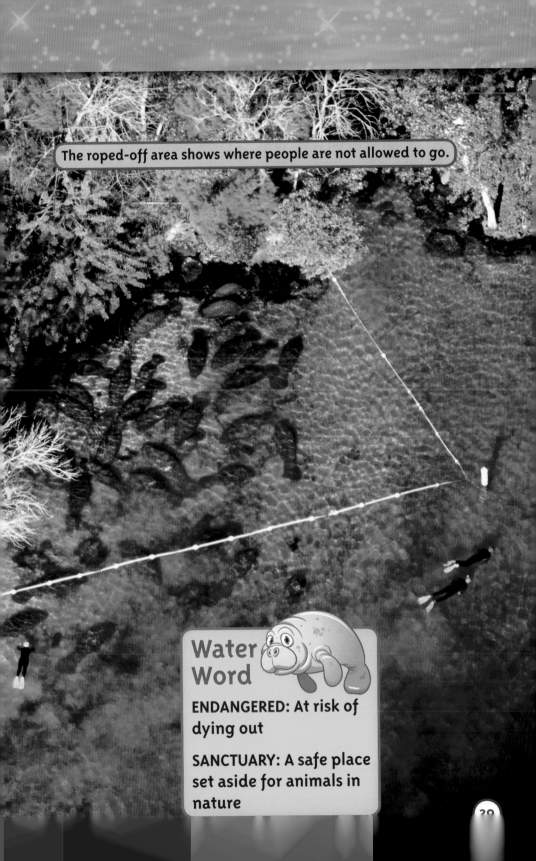

The roped-off area shows where people are not allowed to go.

Water Word

ENDANGERED: At risk of dying out

SANCTUARY: A safe place set aside for animals in nature

Stump Your Parents

Can your parents answer these questions about manatees? You might know more than they do!

Answers at bottom of page 31.

Where do manatees live?
A. In cool, refreshing water
B. In warm, shallow water
C. In deep, warm water
D. On the beach

A baby manatee is called . . .
A. A cub
B. A cow
C. A calf
D. A foal

What do manatees like to eat?
A. Plants
B. Crabs
C. Fruit
D. Steak

4

A manatee's lips . . .

A. Are very small
B. Are perfect for lipstick
C. Get in the way when eating
D. Grab and pull plants into its mouth

5

Manatees rest . . .

A. For many hours
B. For about 30 minutes at a time
C. For about 15 minutes at a time
D. Not at all

6

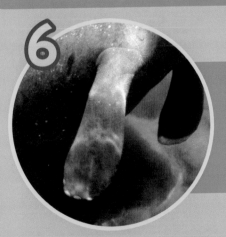

A manatee uses its flippers to . . .

A. Do the backstroke
B. Slap the water
C. Steer through the water
D. Wave to other manatees

7

To keep manatees safe, people should NOT . . .

A. Bother manatees in any way
B. Drive boats really fast
C. Throw trash in the water
D. Do any of the above

ENDANGERED: At risk of dying out

GRAZE: To feed in an area covered with grasses

HERBIVORE: An animal that eats only plants

MAMMAL: An animal that has a backbone and is warm-blooded. It feeds its babies milk.

MIGRATE: To move from one area to another for food or a mate

SANCTUARY: A safe place set aside for animals in nature

LEVEL 2

Sea Turtles

Laura Marsh

NATIONAL GEOGRAPHIC

Washington, D.C.

For Eliza
—L.F.M.

Published by National Geographic Partners, LLC, Washington, DC 20036.

Design by Yay Design

Trade paperback ISBN: 978-1-4263-0853-6
Reinforced library binding ISBN: 978-1-4263-0854-3

Cover, Masa Ushioda/Cool Water Photo; 1, Carson Ganci/Design Pics/Corbis; 2, Frans Lanting;
4-5, Aquascopic/Alamy Stock Photo; 6-7, Jason Isley, Scubazoo/Getty Images; 8, Jason Isley,
Scubazoo/Getty Images; 10, Mark Conlin/V&W/Image Quest Marine; 11 (UP), Doug Perrine/Blue
Planet Archive; 11 (LO), Luiz Claudio Marigo/Nature Picture Library; 12 (UP), James D. Watt/Blue Planet
Archive; 12 (LO), George Burba/Shutterstock; 13 (UP), Doug Perrine/Blue Planet Archive; 13 (LO), Kelvin
Aitkin/V&W/Image Quest Marine; 14, Doug Perrine/Nature Picture Library; 15, Mitsuaki Iwago/Minden
Pictures; 16, Wild Wonders of Europe/Zankl/Nature Picture Library; 18, Jason Bradley; 20, Doug
Perrine/Nature Picture Library; 21, Frans Lemmens/Getty Images; 22, Luciano Candisani/Minden
Pictures; 23 (UP), Nils Bornemann/iStockphoto; 23 (LO), Norbert Wu/Getty Images; 24, Jeffrey L.
Rotman/Corbis/Getty Images; 25, Jim Richardson; 26, Julie Dermansky/Corbis; 27, Audubon Institute
of New Orleans; 28, Audubon Institute of New Orleans; 29 (UP), Audubon Institute of New Orleans;
29 (LO), Heather Stanley, Audubon Nature Institute, New Orleans; 30 (UP), Frank and Helena/Getty
Images; 30 (LO), Gorilla/Shutterstock; 31 (UP), hardcoreboy/iStockphoto; 31 (CTR), Stacie Stauff Smith
Photography/Shutterstock; 31 (LO), Tim Platt/Getty Images; 32 (UP LE), Vlue/Shutterstock; 32 (UP RT),
Doug Perrine/Blue Planet Archive; 32 (LE CTR), Wild Wonders of Europe/Zankl/Nature Picture Library;
32 (RT CTR), Mitsuaki Iwago/Minden Pictures; 32 (LO LE), Stephen Frink/Getty Images; 32 (LO RT),
Jason Isley, Scubazoo/Getty Images

Table of Contents

A Sea Turtle!

Green sea turtle

What hatches on land but spends its life in the sea?

What starts out the size of a Ping-Pong ball but can grow up to seven feet long?

A sea turtle!

Ocean World

Leatherback sea turtle

Sea turtles are graceful swimmers in the water. Their flippers move like wings.

Turtle Term

REPTILE: A cold-blooded animal that lays eggs and has a backbone and scaly skin

Sea turtles travel the world in warm ocean waters. They are one of the few reptiles that live in the sea.

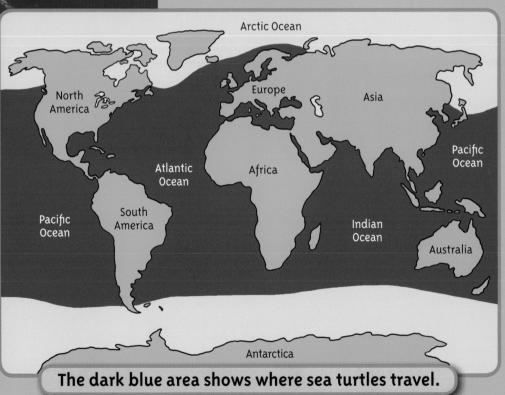

Arctic Ocean

North America

Europe

Asia

Pacific Ocean

Atlantic Ocean

Africa

Pacific Ocean

South America

Indian Ocean

Australia

Antarctica

The dark blue area shows where sea turtles travel.

A sleek body helps
the turtle move easily
through the water.

The scales
on its shell are
called scutes.

The back flippers steer
the turtle as it swims.
They are also used to
dig nests in the sand.

Green sea turtle

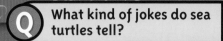
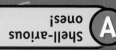
A sea turtle has lungs because it breathes air. A sea turtle holds its breath underwater.

Sea turtles can't pull their heads and limbs into their shells like land turtles can.

Their large, powerful flippers act like paddles.

Scientists believe some sea turtles live 80 years or more, but they don't know for sure.

9

Meet the Turtles!

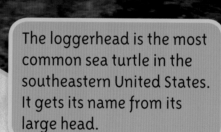

The loggerhead is the most common sea turtle in the southeastern United States. It gets its name from its large head.

There are seven kinds of sea turtles in the world. Each has special features.

The flatback has a flat body. It's the only sea turtle that doesn't live in U.S. waters. It lives near Australia.

The olive ridley has an olive-colored shell. It is shaped like a heart.

The hawksbill can't dive deep. It spends most of its time on the water's surface.

The green turtle has a small head. Unlike other sea turtles, it goes ashore to warm itself in the sun.

The Kemp's ridley likes shallow waters. It's the world's most endangered sea turtle.

Turtle Term

ENDANGERED: At risk of dying out

The leatherback doesn't have a hard shell. Its skin is rubbery with small bones underneath.

Nestbuilding

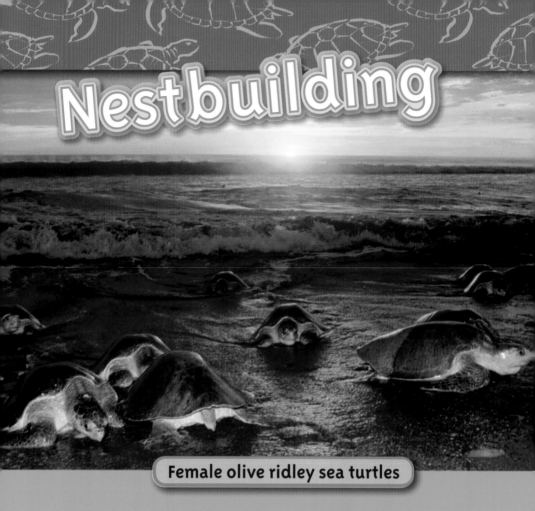

Female olive ridley sea turtles

A female sea turtle comes on land to lay her eggs. She usually returns to the same beach where she hatched.

Scientists aren't sure how sea turtles know where to go. They think sea turtles know by instinct.

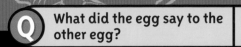

The sea turtle digs a hole with her back flippers. She lays her eggs and covers them with sand. Then she returns to the sea.

Turtle Term

INSTINCT: Behavior that animals are born knowing how to do

Female green sea turtle

15

Oh, Baby!

CRAAACK! The eggs hatch after 50 to 70 days. Tiny turtles called hatchlings crawl out of their eggshells.

Turtle Term

HATCHLING: A young animal that has just come out of its egg

They are less than
three inches long.

3 INCHES

Baby loggerhead sea turtle hatching from its shell

Hatchlings usually crawl toward the sea at night. In the dark, they are hidden from predators.

The little turtles follow the brightest light. The line where the sky meets the sea is the brightest natural light on a beach.

If the hatchlings follow this light, they will make it to the sea.

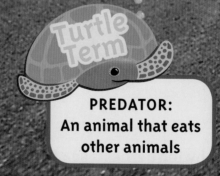

Turtle Term

PREDATOR:
An animal that eats other animals

Q What do you get when you cross a turtle and a porcupine?

A A slowpoke!

Leatherback hatchling

19

Big and Small

The smallest sea turtles are the
Kemp's ridley and the olive ridley.
Adults are about two feet long and
weigh up to 100 pounds.

Kemp's ridley sea turtle

Leatherback sea turtle

The largest sea turtle is the
Leatherback. It can grow up to
seven feet long and weigh more
than 2,000 pounds. That's about
ten men put together!

On the Menu

Green sea turtle

Munch, munch, what's for lunch?

Most sea turtles eat plants and animals.
They dine on algae (AL-gee)
and sea grasses. They
also munch on crab
and conchs.

Turtle Term

ALGAE: Simple,
non-flowering
plants that do not
have stems, roots,
or leaves

Jellyfish are a favorite food for many sea turtles. But plastic trash can look like jellyfish in the ocean, and that spells trouble! Swallowing trash can hurt and even kill sea turtles.

Green sea turtle

Danger!

Hawksbill sea turtle caught in a net

Trash isn't the only danger to sea turtles. Fishing nets and hungry animals can harm them, too.

Building lights confuse hatchlings so they don't reach the sea.

Leatherback sea turtle confused by city lights

Sometimes people even step on sea turtle nests by accident.

Sea Turtle Rescue

In 2010 a giant oil spill leaked into the Gulf of Mexico. Oil covered sea animals and washed up on beaches. Oil is dangerous to people and wildlife.

Oil on beaches in Louisiana

Oil-covered Kemp's ridley

People in charge of a sea turtle rescue program in Louisiana saved many sea turtles.

The rescuers cleaned the turtles and gave them medicine. People cared for them until they could return to the sea.

Kemp's ridley sea turtle

Safekeeping

You don't need to work at a sea turtle hospital to help sea turtles. Here are a few things you can do to keep them safe.

1

Pick up trash on the beach.

2

Don't release balloons into the air. (They often end up in the sea.)

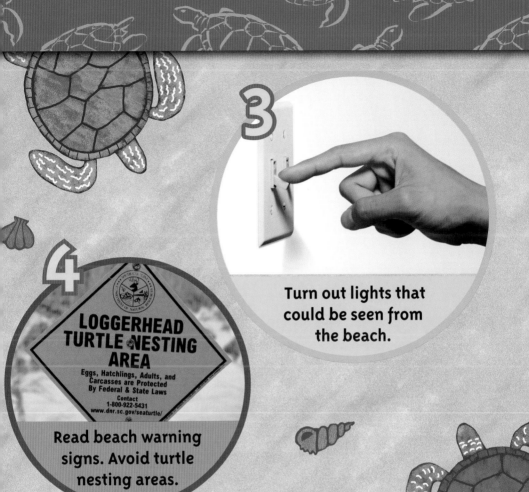

3

Turn out lights that could be seen from the beach.

4

LOGGERHEAD TURTLE NESTING AREA

Eggs, Hatchlings, Adults, and Carcasses are Protected By Federal & State Laws

Contact
1-800-922-5431
www.dnr.sc.gov/seaturtle/

Read beach warning signs. Avoid turtle nesting areas.

5

Tell your classmates what you've learned about sea turtles.

Glossary

ALGAE: Simple, non-flowering plants that do not have stems, roots, or leaves

ENDANGERED: At risk of dying out

HATCHLING: A young animal that has just come out of its egg

INSTINCT: Behavior that animals are born knowing how to do

PREDATOR: An animal that eats other animals

REPTILE: A cold-blooded animal that lays eggs and has a backbone and scaly skin

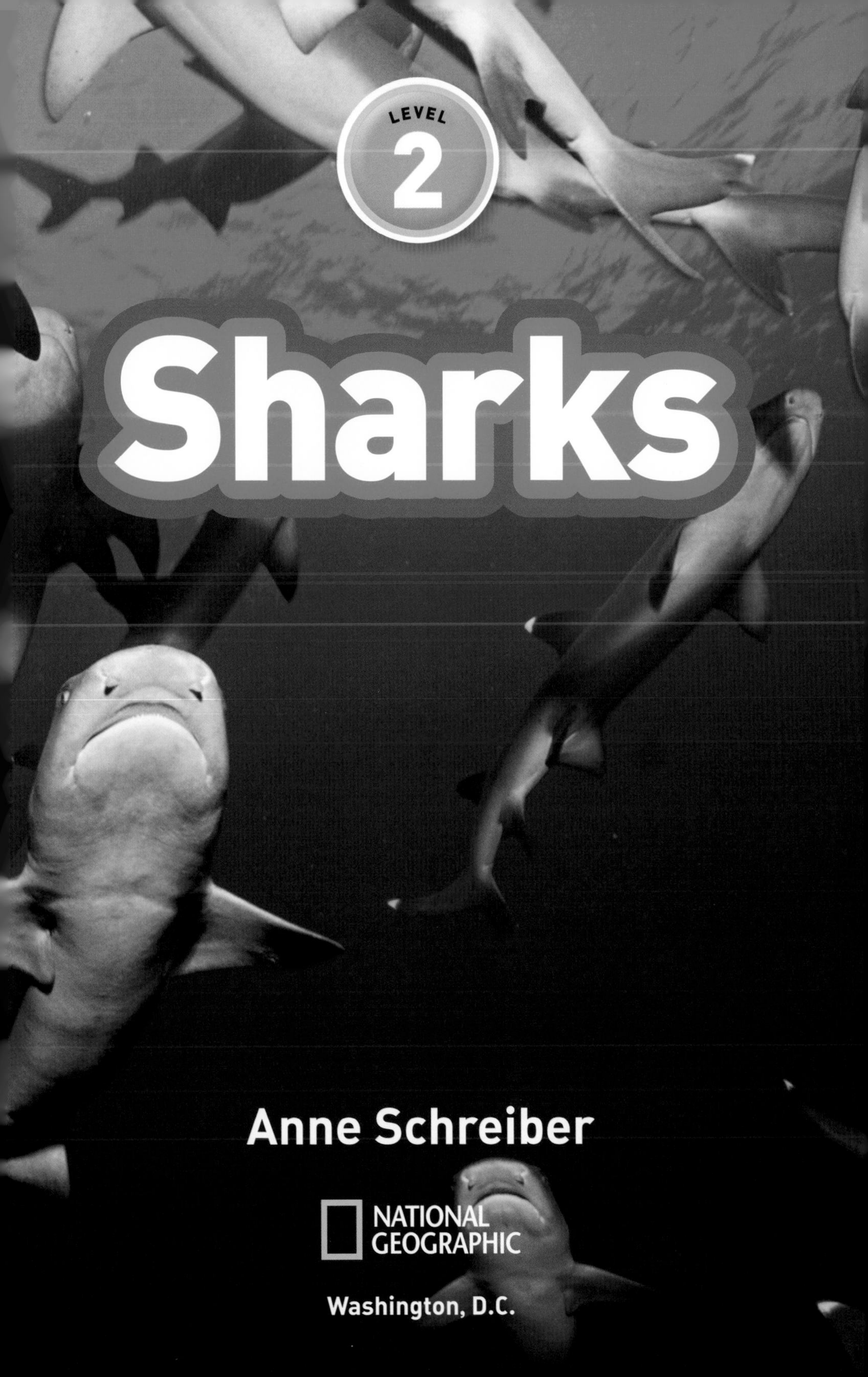

Sharks

Anne Schreiber

NATIONAL GEOGRAPHIC

Washington, D.C.

To Ben, who taught me to love unlovable animals.
—A.S.

Published by National Geographic Partners, LLC, Washington, DC 20036.

Schreiber, Anne.
Sharks! / by Anne Schreiber.
p. cm. — (National Geographic readers)
ISBN 978-1-4263-0286-2 (paperback) — ISBN 978-1-4263-0288-6 (library binding)
1. Sharks--Juvenile literature. I. Title.
QL638.9.S292 2008
597.3—dc22
2007044161

Cover, Tim Davis/Corbis; 1, Jeff Rotman/Blue Planet Archive; 2, Gary Bell/Oceanwide Images; 4-5, David Fleetham/Alamy Stock Photo; 6, Marilyn Barbone/Shutterstock; 6-7, Mark Conlin/V&W/Image Quest Marine; 7, Bob Cranston/Blue Planet Archive; 8-9, Doug Perrine/Blue Planet Archive; 10, Niall Benvie/Nature Picture Library; 11, Mark Conlin/V&W/Image Quest Marine; 12-13, Masa Ushioda/Blue Planet Archive; 14-15, Kike Calvo/Alamy Stock Photo; 16-17, Jeffrey L. Rotman/Blue Planet Archive; 18 (UP), Doug Perrine/Blue Planet Archive; 18 (CTR), Bob Cranston/Blue Planet Archive; 18 (LO), Doug Perrine/Blue Planet Archive; 18 (inset), daily_creativity/Adobe Stock; 19 (UP), Bob Cranston/Blue Planet Archive; 19 (LO), Jeffrey L. Rotman/Blue Planet Archive; 20-21, David Doubilet/National Geographic Image Collection; 22-23 (ribbon), photodisc; 22 (UP), James D. Watt/Blue Planet Archive; 22 (LO), Masa Ushioda/Blue Planet Archive; 23 (UP), C&M Fallows/Blue Planet Archive; 23 (LO), C&M Fallows/Blue Planet Archive; 24-25, Espen Rekdal/Blue Planet Archive; 26-27, Gary Bell/Blue Planet Archive; 28, Steve Robertson - ASP/Covered Images via Getty Images; 29, Noah Hamilton; 30-31, David D. Fleetham/Blue Planet Archive; 32 (UP LE), Mark Conlin/V&W/Image Quest Marine; 32 (UP RT), Jeffrey L. Rotman/Blue Planet Archive; 32 (CTR LE), Masa Ushioda/Blue Planet Archive; 32 (CTR RT), Masa Ushioda/Blue Planet Archive; 32 (LO LE), Bob Cranston/Blue Planet Archive; 32 (LO RT), Doug Perrine/Blue Planet Archive

Table of Contents

CHOMP!

What is quick?
What is quiet?
What has five rows of teeth?
What glides through the water?
CHOMP!
It's a shark!

Sharks live in all of Earth's oceans.
They have been here for a long time.
Sharks were here before dinosaurs.

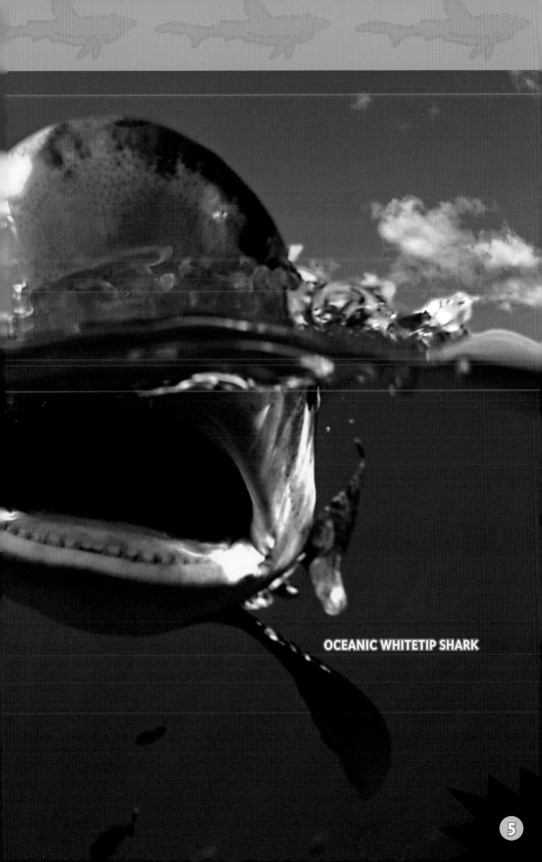

OCEANIC WHITETIP SHARK

CARTILAGE: Cartilage is light, strong, and rubbery. The tip of your nose is cartilage. Can you feel how soft it is?

Shark tail fins are larger on top. This helps them move through the water better.

HAMMERHEAD SHARK

A shark is a fish. But a shark is not like other fish. Sharks do not have bones. They have soft cartilage instead. Cartilage helps sharks twist and turn. Cartilage helps sharks move and bend.

If a shark loses a tooth, a new one moves forward to take its place.

Shark skin feels bumpy and rough. It's hard like sandpaper. It protects sharks and helps them swim faster.

Shark Pups

Shark babies are called pups. Some pups grow inside their mothers. Other pups hatch from eggs.

LEMON SHARK

Lemon shark pups grow inside their mothers. The lemon shark mother goes to shallow water to give birth. The pups stay near the shallow water until they are grown.

These fish are called remoras. They hang around sharks and eat their leftovers.

LEMON SHARK PUP

9

MERMAID'S PURSE

Swell shark pups hatch from eggs. The mother sharks lay the eggs in hard cases. People call the case a mermaid's purse.

A pup coming out of its egg case.

SWELL SHARK PUP

Swell shark mothers lay up to five egg cases at a time. In nine months, the swell shark pups are born.

Pups Grow Up

NURSE SHARK

WORD BITES

PREDATORS: Animals that eat other animals.
PREY: Animals that are eaten by other animals.

When shark pups grow up, they are awesome predators. They have many ways to sense their prey. Did you know a shark can smell blood from miles away? It can smell one drop of blood in 25 million drops of ocean.

Sharks can see better than humans can. Even in deep, dark water, a shark can see its prey.

Sharks take a test bite of prey before eating. Their taste buds tell them if the prey is fat enough to eat.

GREAT WHITE SHARK

15

What Big TEETH You Have

SAND TIGER SHARK

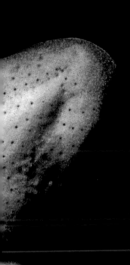

Sharks have many rows of teeth.
They are always losing some teeth.
They are always growing new teeth.
A shark uses up more than 10,000
teeth in its life.

Different sharks have different teeth.
Their teeth are perfect for what they eat.

Long, spiky teeth are
for catching.

Flat teeth are for
grinding.

Serrated teeth are
for ripping.

PREHISTORIC: Prehistoric is a time before people wrote things down.
EXTINCT: Extinct plants and animals are no longer alive on Earth.

MEGALODON TOOTH

Wow! Prehistoric sharks had really big teeth—up to six inches!

The megalodon is a prehistoric shark. Scientists made a life-sized model of the megalodon's jaw and put in the teeth they have found. You can imagine how big the shark must have been.

Imagine This!

A giant shark is gliding through
the water.
A swimmer is nearby.
The shark gets closer.
It is huge.
It opens its giant mouth and...

WHALE SHARK

…sucks in a big mouthful of water.
The swimmer is fine.
The shark is a whale shark.
Whale sharks are the biggest sharks.
But they have tiny teeth.
They eat tiny animals called plankton.

Blue-Ribbon Sharks

There are about 375 different types of sharks.

1ST PLACE

WEIRDEST
The Hammerhead Shark

A hammerhead shark has a head shaped like a giant hammer. Its wide head is great for hunting.

1ST PLACE

The spined pygmy shark is about eight inches long. It has a glow-in-the-dark belly.

SMALLEST
The Spined Pygmy Shark

When a great white bites its prey, its eyes roll back into its head. This protects its eyes.

CREEPIEST
The Great White Shark

The mako is the fastest shark. It can swim up to 20 miles per hour. Makos leap clear out of the water to catch prey.

FASTEST
The Mako Shark

Now You See Them...

LANTERN SHARK

Some sharks glow in the dark! Do you see something shiny in the water? Watch out! The tiny lantern shark is covered with a glow-in-the-dark slime.

The lantern shark is a deep-sea shark. Many deep-sea animals glow. Scientists think glowing might help predators attract prey.

...Now You Don't

Most sharks are hard to see. They have a dark back. From above, they blend in with the water. They have a white belly. From below, they blend in with the sky.

WOBBEGONG SHARK

Some sharks have special ways to hide. Wobbegongs have colors like the seafloor. Their mouths have parts that look like seaweed. Fish swim in but they can't get out!

Shark Attack!

One day Bethany Hamilton went surfing. Suddenly, a tiger shark attacked. It tugged her as she held onto her surfboard. It took a big bite out of her surfboard. It also took Bethany's left arm.

After the attack, Bethany wanted to keep surfing. She is not afraid to go in the water. She knows that shark attacks are rare.

Bethany says, "One thing hasn't changed — and that's how I feel when I'm riding a wave."

People Attack?

Shark attacks are scary, and terrible. Sharks can be a danger to people. But people are a bigger danger to sharks. Millions of sharks die in nets set to catch other fish. Others are killed on purpose.

Many types of sharks may become extinct. Sharks have been on Earth for millions of years. Sharks and people need to learn to share the sea.

GRAY REEF SHARK

CARTILAGE
Cartilage is light, strong and rubbery. Shark skeletons are made of cartilage.

EXTINCT
Extinct plants and animals are no longer alive on Earth.

PREDATOR
A predator is an animal that eats other animals.

PREY
Prey are animals that are eaten by other animals.

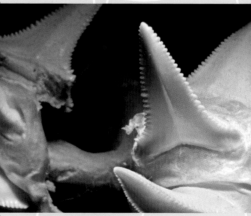

PREHISTORIC
Prehistoric is a time before people wrote things down.

SERRATED
When something is serrated, it has a jagged edge.

Weird Sea Creatures

Laura Marsh

NATIONAL
GEOGRAPHIC
Washington, D.C.

For Finn and Zöe
—L. F. M.

National Geographic gratefully acknowledges the assistance of the National Aquarium.

This material is based upon work supported by the National Science Foundation under Grant No. DRL-1114251. Any opinions, findings, and conclusions or recommendations expressed in this material are those of the author(s) and do not necessarily reflect the views of the National Science Foundation.

As seen on the National Geographic Channel

Published by National Geographic Partners, LLC, Washington, DC 20036.

Design by YAY! Design

Trade paperback ISBN: 978-1-4263-1047-8
Reinforced library binding ISBN: 978-1-4263-1048-5

Table of Contents

Strange But True

balloonfish

Many strange sea creatures live in the ocean.

Some are beautiful. Some are ugly. Some are cute, and some are scary.

Weird sea creatures are strange for a reason. The funny way they look and the strange things they do help them live in the ocean.

Survival Skills

Snorkeling in
shallow water

diagonal butterflyfish

Some sea animals live in the shallow ocean waters. Some live in the deep ocean.

The ocean can be a hard place to live. Deep areas are cold and dark. It can be hard to find food.

And the ocean can be dangerous. There are many predators. Any animal can quickly become dinner for another animal.

Water Word

PREDATOR: An animal that hunts and eats other animals

Sea creatures have special skills that help them find food. They also have strange body parts that can help them hide and stay safe from other animals.

How weird are these sea creatures? Let's find out!

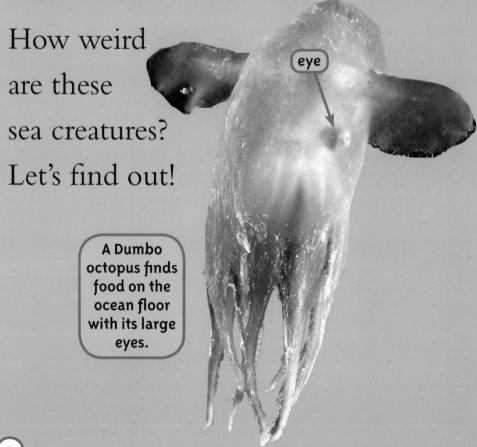

eye

A Dumbo octopus finds food on the ocean floor with its large eyes.

A leafy sea dragon blends in with the seaweed around it.

A moray eel's sharp teeth catch prey.

Hide and Seek

Camouflage (KAM-uh-flazh) helps animals hide from their enemies. Looking strange helps them blend in to the plants or water around them.

Camouflage also helps animals catch dinner. Do you see the stonefish in the picture? Most fish don't because it looks like rock or coral. When they swim too close, the stonefish springs from the ocean floor. It grabs dinner in a flash.

Water Word
CAMOUFLAGE: An animal's natural color or form that blends in with what is around it

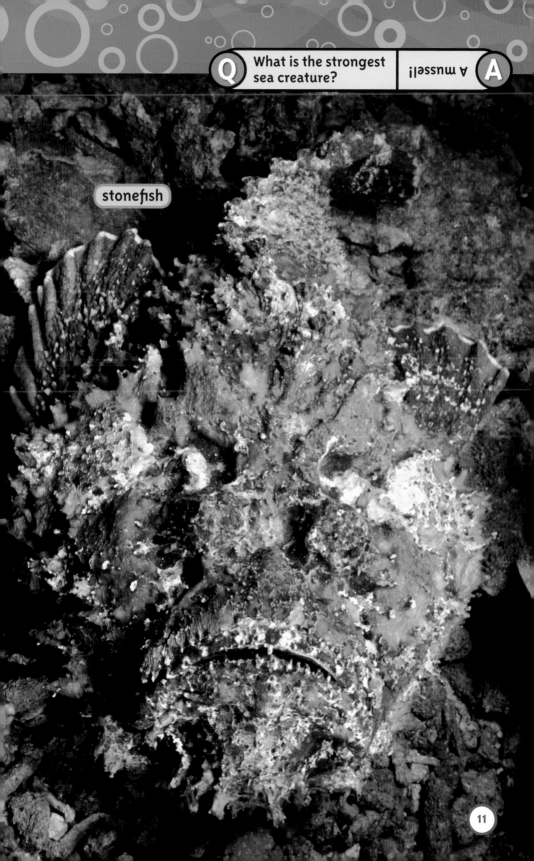

stonefish

Big Eyes

The deep ocean gets very little light. Many animals that live there have large eyes. Big eyes help creatures see in the darkness and find prey.

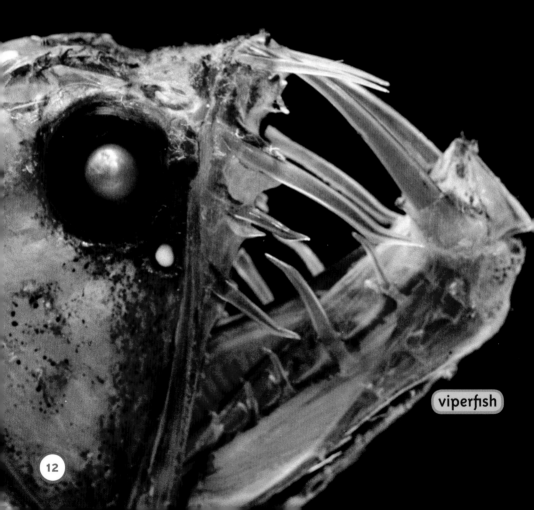

viperfish

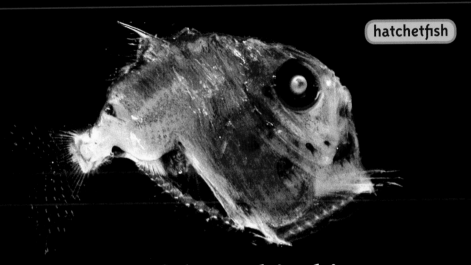

hatchetfish

This viperfish used its big eyes to spot a hatchetfish. Dinnertime!

The hatchetfish uses its own large eyes to find tiny shrimp to eat in the dark sea.

Making Light

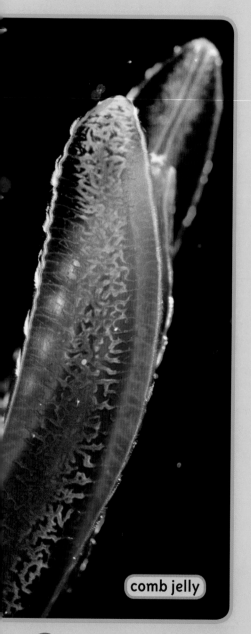

comb jelly

Many creatures in the deep, dark sea have a special trick—they make their own light! This is called bioluminescence (BYE-oh-loom-i-NESS-ants).

Water Word

BIOLUMINESCENCE: Light that an animal makes by itself

The black dragonfish has funny patches that glow in many places on its body.

Some sea creatures use their own light as a flashlight to find prey. Light can draw prey toward an animal, too. And light can surprise enemies, so an animal can make a quick escape.

patch that glows

Expert Food Finders

Some animals have wacky body parts that help them catch meals.

mouth

gulper eel

The gulper eel has a super-long tail. Prey comes closer for a better look. This eel's giant mouth opens wide. It can eat an animal bigger than it is. It can't be picky. In the deep sea, the eel must eat whatever it can find.

tail

The tiny cookie-cutter shark locks onto its prey with strange sucking lips. Its sharp teeth sink in. They leave a bite the shape of a circle.

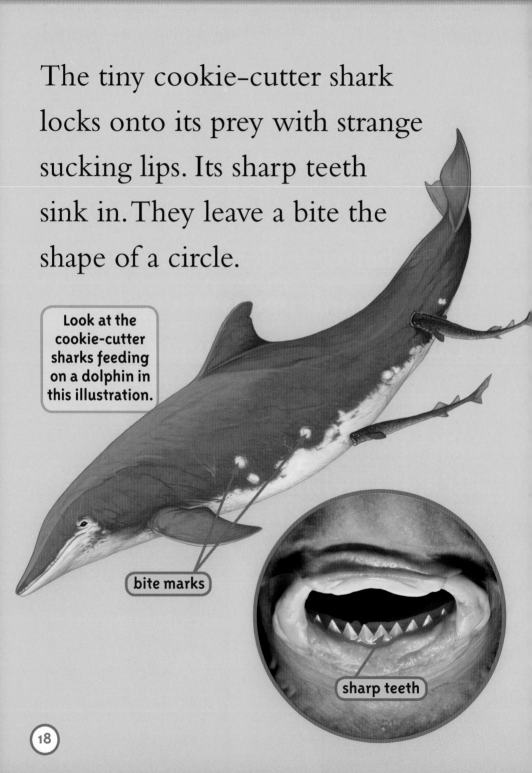

Look at the cookie-cutter sharks feeding on a dolphin in this illustration.

bite marks

sharp teeth

fishing lure

anglerfish

An anglerfish has its own fishing pole called a lure. The lure glows, and other fish want to know what it is. When they get close, the anglerfish eats them.

Deadly Dangers

Bumping into some sea creatures can be bad news.

The yellow sea anemone (ah-NEM-oh-nee) looks like a pretty flower. But it has stinging parts that have deadly venom. When a fish is stung, its muscles stop working. Then the anemone eats the fish.

yellow sea anemone

Water Word

VENOM: A liquid some animals make that can cause stinging, pain, or death

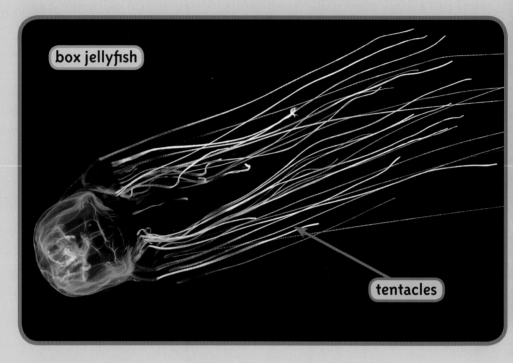

box jellyfish

tentacles

The box jellyfish is one of
the most dangerous animals in
the world. It has arms called
tentacles (TEN-tah-kullz) that
grow up to ten feet long.
The tentacles deliver a painful,
deadly sting.

This lionfish has crazy spiky fins. But you wouldn't want to touch them. The fins on its back are sharp and can sting you.

fins with venom

lionfish

Strange Senses

Some animals near the ocean floor don't even have eyes! They can't see their food. So they use other senses to find it.

A sea cucumber can feel tiny pieces of food stuck to its tube feet. It curls its feet in and licks them clean.

sea cucumber

hagfish

A hagfish has a super strong sense of smell and touch. It can smell food that's fallen from higher up in the ocean. It also uses feelers to find meals.

Super Subs!

How do we know about weird sea creatures in the deep ocean?

People can't dive deep to see these strange creatures. It's too cold and dark there. And the water pressure is strong enough to crush a person.

But humans can use machines called submersibles (sub-MER-sih-bullz) to explore the deep ocean.

Sometimes people control them from far away, like a remote-controlled car. And sometimes people ride inside.

14,764 feet

How Deep?

This submersible, named Alvin, can dive 14,764 feet deep. It would take more than 10 Empire State Buildings stacked up to reach that depth.

These odd tube worms live on the bottom of the ocean. They can grow to be eight feet tall.

Submersibles collect information. They have lights and special tools. They take pictures, and they gather plants, rocks, and animals.

Scientists used submersibles to find the weird creatures shown here. And there are probably thousands more that have not been found yet.

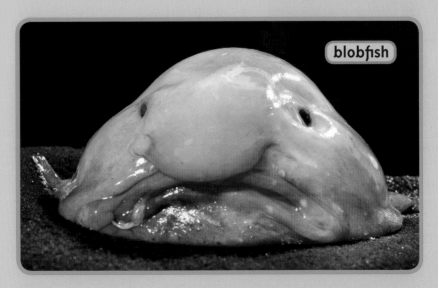

blobfish

Stump Your Parents

Can your parents answer these questions about sea creatures? You might know more than they do!

Answers are at the bottom of page 31.

1

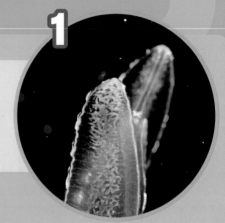

Bioluminescence is ____.

A. a loud sound
B. the light an animal makes
C. a search for food
D. a fast swim

2

Machines that dive deep in the ocean are called ____.

A. speedboats
B. planes
C. submersibles
D. scuba suits

3

Which features are common in deep-sea animals?

A. big mouth
B. big teeth
C. big eyes
D. all of the above

4

Animals that have venom are _____.

A. not harmful
B. friendly
C. able to cause stinging, pain, or death
D. only found in shallow waters

5

Humans can't scuba dive deep into the ocean because _____.

A. it's too cold
B. it's too dark
C. the pressure is too great
D. all of the above

6

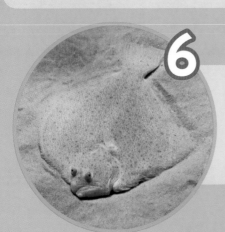

What is camouflage?

A. a way of eating
B. a way to blend in and hide
C. how animals see in the dark
D. none of the above

7

An animal that is eaten by another animal is called _____.

A. prey
B. an anemone
C. a tentacle
D. a creature

BIOLUMINESCENCE: Light that an animal makes by itself

CAMOUFLAGE: An animal's natural color or form that blends in with what is around it

PREDATOR: An animal that hunts and eats other animals

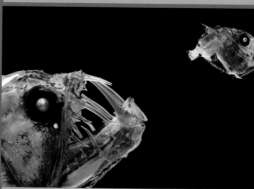

PREY: An animal that is eaten by another animal

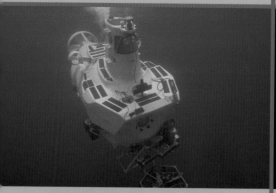

SUBMERSIBLE: An underwater craft used to explore and gather information

VENOM: A liquid some animals make that can cause stinging, pain, or death